Measuring Time

# Seasons of the Year

Tracey Steffora

KU-220-352

Raintree

**www.raintreepublishers.co.uk**
Visit our website to find out more information about Raintree books.

**To order:**
☎ Phone 0845 6044371
🖨 Fax +44 (0) 1865 312263
✉ Email myorders@raintreepublishers.co.uk

Customers from outside the UK please telephone +44 1865 312262

Raintree is an imprint of Capstone Global Library Limited, a company incorporated in England and Wales having its registered office at 7 Pilgrim Street, London, EC4V 6LB – Registered company number: 6695582

Edited by Tracey Steffora, Dan Nunn, and Sian Smith
Designed by Richard Parker
Picture research by Hannah Taylor
Originated by Capstone Global Library Ltd
Printed and bound in China by Leo Paper Products Ltd

ISBN 978 1 406 22302 6
15 14 13 12 11
10 9 8 7 6 5 4 3 2 1

**British Library Cataloguing in Publication Data**
Steffora, Tracey.
    Seasons of the year. -- (Measuring time)
    1. Seasons--Juvenile literature. 2. Time--Juvenile literature.
    I. Title II. Series
    508.2-dc22

**Acknowledgements**
We would like to thank the following for permission to reproduce photographs: Alamy Images pp. **4** (©Cultura), **15** (©RubberBall), **22 top right** (©Jon Helgason); Corbis pp. **5** (epa/Kay Nietfeld), **21** (Blend Images/Jamie Grill/JGI); istockphoto pp. **6** (©Ermin Gultenberger), **14** (©LeoGrand), **16** (©Primary Picture), **19** (©Morley Read), **22 bot** (©mammamaart), **22 top left** (©David Safanda); NASA p. **23 top**; Photolibrary pp. **10** (Comstock), **18** (Superstock); shutterstock pp. **7** (©Kai Schirmer), **8** (©Foto Yakov), **11** (©Nagel Photography), **12** (©RazvanZinica), **13** (©Shebeko), **17** (©Dennis Donohue), **20** (©Graeme Dawes), **23 bot** (oriontrail).

Front cover photographs of sunflowers reproduced with permission of Alamy Images (©David Norton Photograghy), autumn leaves reproduced with permission of Alamy Images (©Bob Handelman), frosted pine needles reproduced with permission of Alamy Images (©Christina Bollen) and tree bud reproduced with permission of Photolibrary (Mixa). Back cover photograph of a person sliding down a snowy hill reproduced with permission of istockphoto (© Ermin Gultenberger).

Every effort has been made to contact copyright holders of any material reproduced in this book. Any omissions will be rectified in subsequent printings if notice is given to the publisher.

# Contents

# Time and seasons

Time is how long something takes.

5

Time is when things happen.

Some things take a short time.
Some things take a long time.

A season is a long amount of time.

spring

summer

autumn

winter

There are four seasons in one year.

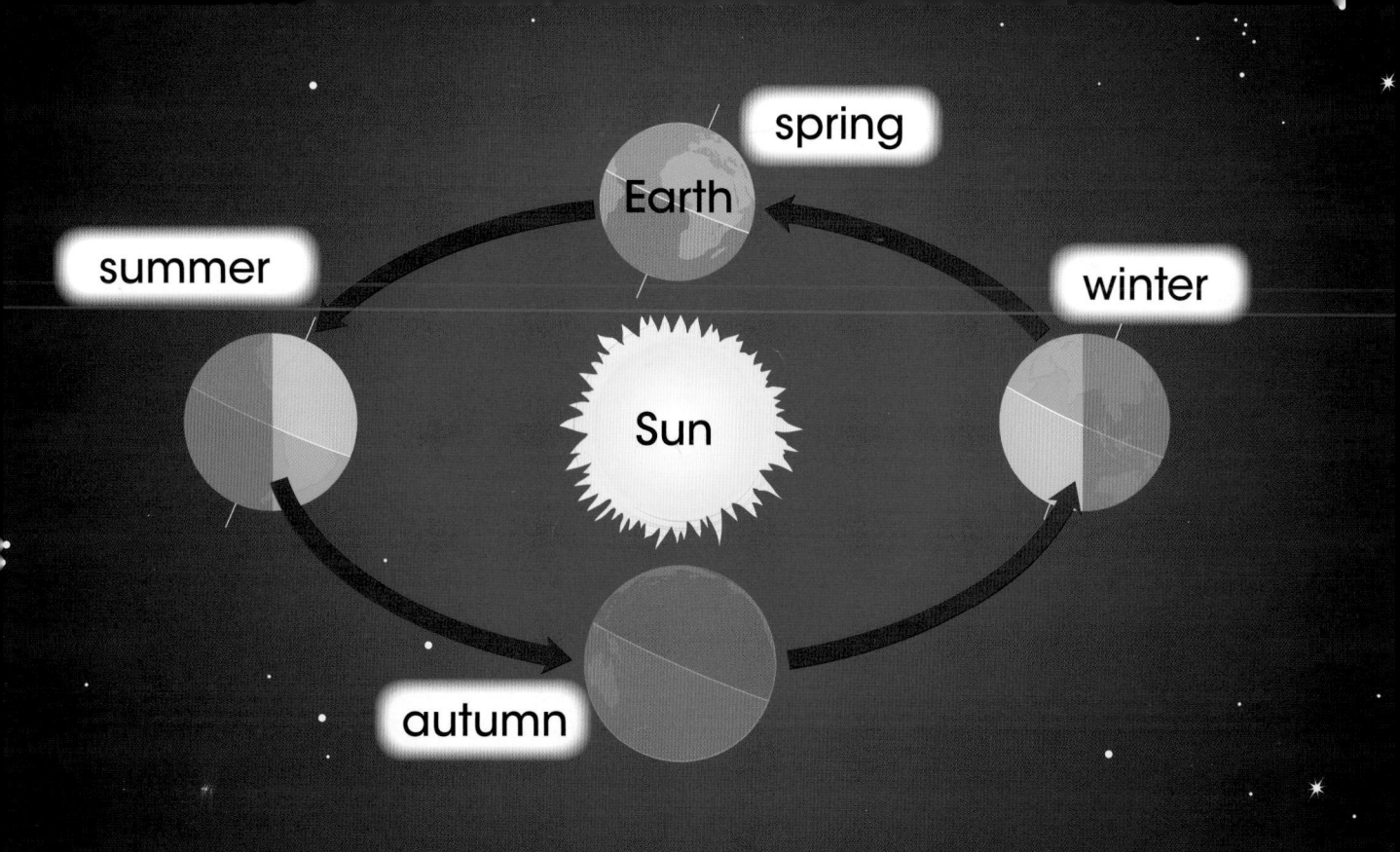

The seasons change as the Earth travels around the Sun.

# Winter

In winter we feel the cold.

In winter we taste hot chocolate.

In winter we hear the wind.

In winter we see trees with no leaves.

# Spring

In spring we feel warm weather.

In spring we hear birds sing.

In spring we see new plants.

In spring we smell flowers.

# Summer

In summer we feel the heat.

In summer we see the bright Sun.

In summer we see people in shorts.

In summer we hear water splash.

# Autumn

In autumn we feel cool weather.

In autumn we hear leaves crunch.

In autumn we see birds flying south.
In autumn we see leaves changing colour.

# Around the world

Some places are always cold.

Some places are always hot.

We use a calendar to know the season.

see    hear    feel    taste    smell

We use our senses to know the season.

What are the seasons like where you live?

# Picture glossary

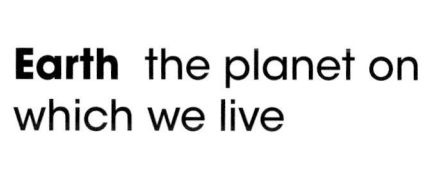

**Earth** the planet on which we live

**Sun** the star that gives heat and light to the Earth. The Earth moves around the Sun.

# Index

**Notes for parents and teachers**
**Before reading**
Ask the children about the current season. Discuss what the characteristics of that season are like where you live. Prompt children to think about the different clothing they might wear during different seasons. Review the five senses with children and begin a discussion of things that they might see, hear, smell, feel, and taste in each season.

**After reading**
Collect photos that illustrate different seasons or encourage the children to bring in pictures they have collected themselves. Use these pictures for a sorting activity.